Cool
East Coast Cooking

Easy and Fun Regional Recipes

Alex Kuskowski

visit us at www.abdopublishing.com

Published by ABDO Publishing Company, a division of ABDO, P.O. Box 398166, Minneapolis, Minnesota 55439. Copyright © 2014 by Abdo Consulting Group, Inc. International copyrights reserved in all countries. No part of this book may be reproduced in any form without written permission from the publisher. Super SandCastle™ is a trademark and logo of ABDO Publishing Company.

Printed in the United States of America, North Mankato, Minnesota
062013
092013

Editor: Liz Salzmann
Content Developer: Nancy Tuminelly
Cover and Interior Design and Production:
Colleen Dolphin, Mighty Media, Inc.
Food Production: Desirée Bussiere

Photo Credits: Colleen Dolphin, Shutterstock

The following manufacturers/names appearing in this book are trademarks: Brer Rabbit®, Chicken of the Sea®, Old London®, Quaker®, Roundy's®, Snow's® Bumble Bee®

Library of Congress Cataloging-in-Publication Data

Kuskowski, Alex.
  Cool East Coast cooking : easy and fun regional recipes / Alex Kuskowski.
      pages cm. -- (Cool USA cooking)
  Audience: Age 4-12.
  Includes index.
  ISBN 978-1-61783-828-6
  1. Cooking, American--Juvenile literature.
  2. Cooking--East (U.S.)--Juvenile literature.
  3. Cooking--Atlantic Coast (U.S.)--Juvenile literature.
  I. Title.
  TX715.K945 2013
  641.5974--dc23
                                    2013001856

Safety First!

Some recipes call for activities or ingredients that require caution. If you see these symbols ask an adult for help!

HOT STUFF!
This recipe requires the use of a stove or oven. Always use pot holders when handling hot objects.

SUPER SHARP!
This recipe includes the use of a sharp **utensil** such as a knife or grater.

Cuisine Cooking

Each regional recipe can have a lot of **versions**. Many are **unique** to the cook. The recipes in this book are meant to give you just a taste of regional cooking. If you want to learn more about one kind of cooking, go to your local library or search online. There are many great recipes to try!

Contents

Discover East Coast Eats!

Get ready to make some great East Coast foods! The East Coast is home to a lot of famous dishes. Have you ever tried pancakes and maple syrup, a spoonful of baked beans, or a Philly cheesesteak **sandwich**? They are just some of the tasty eats from the East Coast.

Many people know East Coast recipes because they have been around for hundreds of years. When the Pilgrims arrived in America in the 1600s they had to learn how to cook with the ingredients nearby. The East Coast has good farmland. It is also close to the ocean. It was easy to get fruit, **seafood**, and vegetables. Many Pilgrims got together to share their food at feasts.

There is a lot to learn about foods from the East Coast. Use the recipes in this book to have your own feast. Try them all, or make up your own. Grab a chef's hat, it's time for a cooking adventure!

Learn About the East Coast

Regional cooking has a lot to do with where the ingredients and recipes are from. Every region has its own **culture**. What do you know about East Coast culture and food?

Rhode Island

Rhode Island has a lot of clambakes where they eat a local favorite, clam cakes.

New Jersey

Salt water **taffy** is one of the most famous East Coast treats. It was first made in Atlantic City.

Connecticut

Lollipops were first made in New Haven, Connecticut, in 1908. They were named after a racehorse.

Massachusetts

The first Thanksgiving was celebrated in Plymouth in 1621.

New Hampshire

A company in Manchester baked what was once the largest **cupcake** in the world. The cupcake was 1,224 pounds, used 800 eggs, and took 12 hours to bake.

Vermont

Vermont is the state that makes the most maple syrup. They make 500,000 **gallons** a year. All that syrup goes great with pancakes!

Delaware

Delaware has a soft spot for peach pie. It's their state **dessert**.

Pennsylvania

Hershey, Pennsylvania, is the home of Hershey's chocolate.

Maryland

Maryland is known for crab cakes. Many people catch and cook their own crabs as a special treat!

Maine

In 1848 chewing gum was invented in Bangor, Maine. It was made from the sap of a spruce tree.

New York

The biggest city in the country is New York City. One nickname for the city is "The Big Apple." It inspired New Yorkers to make the apple the state fruit.

The Basics

Ask Permission

Before you cook, ask **permission** to use the kitchen, cooking tools, and ingredients. If you'd like to do something yourself, say so. Just remember to be safe. If you would like help, ask for it. Always ask for help using a stove or oven.

Be Prepared

- Be organized. Knowing where everything is makes cooking easier and safer.

- Read the directions all the way through before you start. Remember to follow the directions in order.

- The most important ingredient in great cooking is preparation! Set out all your ingredients before starting.

Be Neat and Clean

- Start with clean hands, clean tools, and a clean work surface.

- Tie back long hair so it stays out of the food.

- Wear comfortable clothing. Roll up long sleeves.

Be Smart, Be Safe

- Never work in the kitchen if you are home alone.

- Always have an adult close by for hot jobs, such as using the oven or the stove.

- Have an adult around when using a sharp tool, such as a knife or grater. Always be careful when using them!

- Remember to turn pot handles toward the back of the stove. That way you won't accidentally knock them over.

Cool Cooking Terms

Peel

Peel means to remove the skin, often with a peeler.

Chop

Chop means to cut into small pieces.

Boil

Boil means to heat liquid until it begins to bubble.

Dice / Cube

Dice and *cube* mean to cut something into small squares.

Slice

Slice means to cut food into pieces of the same thickness.

Grate

Grate means to shred something into small pieces using a grater.

Whisk

Whisk means to beat quickly by hand with a whisk or a fork.

Mince

Mince means to cut or chop into very small pieces.

The Tool Box

Here are some of the tools that you'll need for the recipes in this book.

8 × 8-inch baking dish

baking sheet

frying pan

electric mixer

loaf pan

measuring cups & spoons

mixing bowls

peeler

pot holders

rubber spatula

saucepan

whisk

The Ingredients

Here are some of the ingredients that you'll need for the recipes in this book.

bacon

bread crumbs

butter

canned clams

clam juice

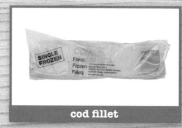
cod fillet

dark molasses

dried thyme

grated Parmesan cheese

green beans

green pepper

ground allspice

ground cinnamon

ground ginger

ground nutmeg

hoagie buns

maple syrup

mushrooms

olive oil

onion

paprika

potatoes

processed cheddar cheese

pumpkin puree

red pepper

rib-eye steak

yellow cornmeal

13

Johnnycake Breakfast

Wake up to this sweet cornmeal treat!

Makes 6 servings

Ingredients

non-stick cooking spray
1½ cups yellow cornmeal
1½ cups flour
½ cup sugar
3 teaspoons baking powder
½ teaspoon salt
2 tablespoons butter
1 egg
1½ cups milk
1 cup maple syrup

Tools

8 × 8-inch baking dish
measuring cups
measuring spoons
large mixing bowl
mixing spoon
small bowl
rubber spatula
pot holders
dinner knife

*hot!

1 Preheat the oven to 375 degrees. Coat the baking dish with cooking spray.

2 Put the cornmeal, flour, sugar, baking powder, and salt in a large bowl. Stir.

3 Put the butter in a small bowl. Heat in the microwave for 10 seconds.

4 Add the butter, egg, and milk to the cornmeal mixture. Stir until the lumps disappear.

5 Pour the mixture into the baking dish. Smooth it with a rubber spatula.

6 Bake for 30 minutes. Remove from oven. Cut into squares and serve hot with maple syrup.

Creamy Clam Chowder

You will be clam-oring for more!

Makes 4 servings

Ingredients

2 slices bacon, cooked and diced
1½ cups chopped onion
1 teaspoon salt
½ teaspoon dried thyme
1 garlic clove, minced
1½ cups clam juice
5 cups peeled and diced potatoes
2 tablespoons flour
2 (10 ounce) cans chopped clams, with liquid
3 cups half-and-half

Tools

sharp knife
cutting board
measuring cups
measuring spoons
large saucepan
mixing spoon
ladle
serving bowls

*hot!
*sharp!

1. Put the bacon, onion, salt, thyme, and garlic in the saucepan. Cook for 4 minutes, stirring constantly.

2. Add the clam juice and potatoes. Cover and cook for 20 minutes.

3. Add the flour, clams, and half-and-half. Bring to a boil. Stir constantly.

4. Cook about 5 more minutes or until thick. Ladle into bowls for you and your friends!

How to Cook Bacon

1. Put the bacon in a frying pan. Cook on medium heat.

2. Flip the bacon with a fork or tongs after 2 minutes. Cook until bacon is **crispy**, about 5 minutes.

3. Remove the pan from the heat. Set the bacon on paper towels to drain.

Maine Pumpkin Bread

A perfect snack year-round!

Makes 3 loaves

Ingredients

non-stick cooking spray
1 (15-ounce) can
 pumpkin puree
4 eggs
1 cup vegetable oil
3 cups sugar
3½ cups flour
2 teaspoons baking soda
1½ teaspoons salt
1 teaspoon ground cinnamon
1 teaspoon ground nutmeg
½ teaspoon ground cloves
¼ teaspoon ground ginger

Tools

3 loaf pans
measuring cups
measuring spoons
mixing bowls
mixing spoon
whisk
pot holders

1. Preheat the oven to 350 degrees. Coat the loaf pan with cooking spray. Set aside.

2. Put the pumpkin puree, eggs, vegetable oil, sugar, and ⅔ cup water in a large mixing bowl. Stir and set aside.

3. Put the flour, baking soda, salt, cinnamon, nutmeg, cloves, and ginger in a medium mixing bowl. Whisk together.

4. Slowly pour the flour mixture into the pumpkin mixture. Stir well.

5. Fill each loaf pan half full with batter. Bake for 50 minutes. Cool loaves for 10 minutes before serving.

*hot!

Fry-It-Up Fish 'n' Chips

A New England favorite sure to please!

Makes 4 servings

Ingredients

4 potatoes, sliced
2 tablespoons olive oil
½ cup flour
3 eggs
½ cup bread crumbs
¼ cup grated Parmesan cheese
1 teaspoon paprika
1-pound cod fillet,
    cut into bite-sized chunks
4 tablespoons vegetable oil

Tools

baking sheet
basting brush
pot holders
3 mixing bowls
frying pan
measuring cups
measuring spoons
tongs
paper towels
sharp knife
cutting board
grater

*hot!
*sharp!

1 Preheat the oven to 400 degrees.

2 Put the potato slices on the baking sheet. Brush them with olive oil until evenly coated. Bake for 45 minutes. Remove from oven and set aside.

3 Put the flour in one mixing bowl. Put the eggs in the second bowl. Beat them with a fork. Put the bread crumbs, Parmesan, and paprika in the third bowl.

4 Dip each piece of fish into the flour bowl, then the egg bowl, and finally in the bread crumb bowl. Make sure they get completely coated. Set them aside.

5 Heat the vegetable oil in a frying pan over medium heat. Add the fish. After 3 minutes, turn the fish with tongs. Cook another 3 minutes. Put the fish on a paper towel.

6 Serve the fish and chips together. Try it with malt vinegar, lemon, or tartar sauce for extra flavor!

Three Sisters Soup

A savory soup and a tasty tradition!

Makes 6 servings

Ingredients

1 tablespoon olive oil

1 cup diced onion

1 teaspoon garlic salt

2 cups drained canned corn

2 cups green beans

2 cups peeled and cubed yellow squash

1½ cups peeled and cubed potatoes

1 cup of red pepper, diced

1½ tablespoons chicken bouillon granules

2 tablespoons butter, cubed

2 tablespoons flour

½ teaspoon black pepper

½ teaspoon cinnamon

Tools

measuring cups

measuring spoons

frying pan

sharp knife

cutting board

peeler

large saucepan

mixing spoons

small mixing bowl

ladle

serving bowls

*hot!
*sharp!

1. Heat the olive oil, onion, and garlic salt in a frying pan on medium heat. Stir and cook for 5 minutes. Remove from heat and set aside.

2. Put the corn, beans, squash, potatoes, red pepper, and 5 cups water in a large saucepan. Stir in bouillon granules.

3. Heat the vegetable mixture in the saucepan on high until it boils. Cook 10 mintues or until the vegetables are soft. Stir constantly.

4. Mix the flour and butter together in a small bowl. Add it to the saucepan. Stir.

5. Turn the heat to medium. Add the onion mixture. Cook 5 minutes, until the soup thickens. Add the black pepper and cinnamon.

6. Ladle into bowls for a truly traditional feast!

Philly Cheesesteak Sandwich

Wow! Steak and veggies and cheese!

Makes 4 servings

Ingredients

1 tablespoon olive oil

1 teaspoon minced garlic

1 onion, sliced

½ cup sliced green pepper

½ cup sliced mushrooms

½-pound rib-eye steak, thinly sliced

2 hoagie buns, cut lengthwise

1 can processed cheddar cheese

½ teaspoon salt

¼ teaspoon black pepper

Tools

sharp knife

cutting board

measuring cups

measuring spoons

frying pan

mixing spoon

large mixing bowl

tongs

*hot!
*sharp!

1 Put the olive oil, garlic, onion, green pepper, and mushrooms in a frying pan. Cook over medium-high heat for 6 minutes. Stir constantly. Remove the pan from the heat. Put the vegetables in a mixing bowl.

2 Place the frying pan back on the stove. Put the meat in it and cook over medium-high heat. When the meat begins to turn brown, flip it over with tongs. When both sides are brown, add the vegetables.

3 Stir and cook for 2 minutes. Turn off the stove. Use tongs to put some of the steak and vegetable mixture in each hoagie bun.

4 Add cheese to each **sandwich**. Let the cheese melt for 1 minute. Season with salt and black pepper. Cut each sandwich in half. Enjoy this Philadelphia favorite!

Tip: Switch out the processed cheese for Provolone, Sharp Cheddar, or American cheese!

Big Apple Cheesecake

It'll be gone in a New York minute!

Makes 1 cheesecake

Ingredients

non-stick cooking spray

15 graham crackers, crushed

3 tablespoons butter, melted

32 ounces cream cheese, softened

1½ cups sugar

¾ cup milk

4 eggs

1 cup sour cream

1 tablespoon vanilla extract

¼ cup flour

Tools

9-inch round pie plate

mixing bowls

mixing spoon

measuring cups

measuring spoons

electric mixer

pot holders

*hot!

1 Preheat the oven to 350 degrees. Coat the pie plate with cooking spray.

2 Combine graham cracker crumbs and butter in a medium mixing bowl. Stir well. Press the mixture evenly in the bottom of the pie plate. Put it in the freezer.

3 Put the cream cheese and sugar in a large mixing bowl. Beat with mixer for 3 minutes. Mix in the milk.

4 Add 1 egg at a time. Beat with mixer after each egg. Mix in sour cream, vanilla, and flour. Beat well.

5 Remove the crust from the freezer. Pour the cream cheese mixture into the crust. Bake 1 hour.

6 Turn the oven off. Let the cheesecake cool in the oven for 4 hours. Remove from oven. Chill in the refrigerator until ready to serve.

Classy Molasses Cookies

These treats will make your mouth water!

Makes 36 cookies

Ingredients

¾ cup butter
1 egg
1½ cups sugar
¾ cup dark molasses
2 cups flour
1 teaspoon salt
1 teaspoon baking soda
1½ teaspoons ground ginger
½ teaspoon ground cloves
½ teaspoon ground nutmeg
¼ teaspoon ground allspice
non-stick cooking spray

Tools

measuring cups
measuring spoons
mixing bowls
electric mixer
whisk
baking sheet
fork
pot holders

*hot!

1 Put the butter, egg, and 1 cup sugar in a large mixing bowl. Beat with mixer. Add the molasses. Beat until smooth. Set aside.

2 Put the flour, salt, baking soda, ginger, cloves, nutmeg, and allspice in a medium mixing bowl. Whisk them together. Pour the flour mixture into the molasses mixture. Stir well. Put the dough in the refrigerator for 1 hour.

3 Preheat the oven to 375 degrees. Coat the baking sheet with cooking spray.

4 Remove the dough from the refrigerator. Sprinkle flour on your hands. Roll the dough into small balls. Roll each ball in sugar.

5 Place the balls of dough on the baking sheet. Flatten them with a fork. Bake for 12 minutes. Let the cookies cool.

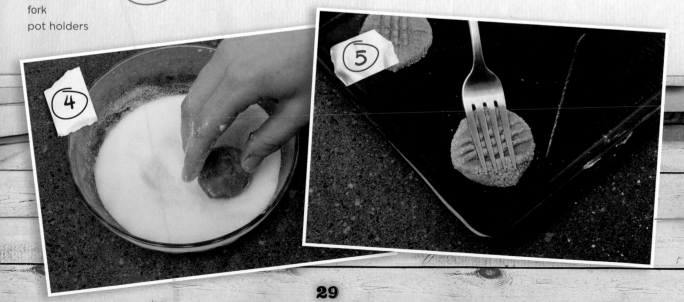

Conclusion

Now you know how to make some wonderful East Coast dishes! Did you learn anything about East Coast **cuisine**? Did you try any new foods? Everywhere you go there are new foods to experience.

From coast to coast the United States is a land of **delicious** dishes! East Coast, Pacific Coast, Gulf Coast, Midwest, South, and West are the main regions of US cuisine. Try them all to get a taste of the United States. See if one is your favorite!

Glossary

culture – the behavior, beliefs, art, and other products of a particular group of people.

crispy – hard, thin, and easy to break.

cuisine – a style of preparing and presenting food.

cupcake – a small cake about the size and shape of a teacup.

delicious – very pleasing to taste or smell.

dessert – a sweet food, such as fruit, ice cream, or pastry, served after a meal.

gallon – a unit for measuring liquids. Milk and gasoline are often sold by the gallon.

lollipop – a piece of hard candy on the end of a stick.

permission – when a person in charge says it's okay to do something.

sandwich – two pieces of bread with a filling, such as meat, cheese, or peanut butter, between them.

seafood – edible fish and shellfish, such as trout, salmon, clams, and lobster.

taffy – a candy usually made with molasses or brown sugar that is boiled and pulled until chewy.

unique – different, unusual, or special.

utensil – a tool used to prepare or eat food.

version – a different form or type from the original.

Web Sites

To learn more about regional US cooking, visit ABDO Publishing Company online at www.abdopublishing.com. Web sites about easy and fun regional recipes are featured on our Book Links page. These links are routinely monitored and updated to provide the most current information available.

Index